# NEIGHBORHOOD ODES

OTHER BOOKS BY GARY SOTO

*Baseball in April and Other Stories*
*Taking Sides*

# GARY SOTO
# NEIGHBORHOOD
# ODES

*Illustrated by*
DAVID DIAZ

**HARCOURT BRACE & COMPANY**
Orlando  Atlanta  Austin  Boston  San Francisco  Chicago  Dallas  New York
Toronto  London

This edition is published by special arrangement with Harcourt Brace
& Company.

*Neighborhood Odes* by Gary Soto, illustrated by David Diaz. Text copyright
© 1992 by Gary Soto; illustrations copyright © 1992 by Harcourt Brace
& Company. Reprinted by permission of Harcourt Brace & Company.

Printed in the United States of America

ISBN 0-15-302259-0

2 3 4 5 6 7 8 9 10   071   97 96 95 94 93

# CONTENTS

# NEIGHBORHOOD ODES

# ODE TO LOS RASPADOS

Papá says
They were
A shiny dime
When he was
Little, but for me,
His daughter
With hair that swings
Like jump ropes,
They're free:
Papá drives a truck
Of *helados* and
Snow cones, the
Music of arrival
Playing block
After block.
It's summer now.
The sun is bright
As a hot dime.
You need five
Shiny ones
For a snow cone:
Strawberry and root beer,
Grape that stains
The mouth with laughter,
Orange that's a tennis ball
Of snow
You could stab
With a red-striped straw.
We have

Green lime
And dark cola,
And we have
An umbrella of five colors.
When the truck stops,
The kids come running,
Some barefoot,
Some in T-shirts
That end at the
Cyclone knot
Of belly buttons,
Some in swimming
Trunks and dripping
Water from a sprinkler
On a brown lawn.
I'm twelve going
On thirteen,
And I know what's what
When it comes to
Snow cones
Packed with the flat
Of a hand and laced
With a gurgle
Of sugary water.
I know the rounds
Of the neighborhood.
I know the kids,
Gina and Ofélia,
Juan and Ananda,
Shorty and Sleepy,
All running
With dimes pressed
To their palms,
Salted from play

Or mowing the lawn.
When they walk away,
The dime of sun
Pays them back
With laughter
And the juice runs
To their elbows,
Sticky summer rain
That sweetens the street.

# ODE TO LA TORTILLA

They are flutes
When rolled, butter
Dripping down my elbow
As I stand on the
Front lawn, just eating,
Just watching a sparrow
Hop on the lawn,
His breakfast of worms
Beneath the green, green lawn,
Worms and a rip of
Tortilla I throw
At his thorny feet.
I eat my tortilla,
Breathe in, breathe out,
And return inside,
Wiping my oily hands
On my knee-scrubbed jeans.
The tortillas are still warm
In a dish towel,
Warm as gloves just
Taken off, finger by finger.
Mamá is rolling
Them out. The radio
On the window sings,
*El cielo es azul* . . .
I look in the black pan:
The face of the tortilla
With a bubble of air
Rising. Mamá

Tells me to turn
It over, and when
I do, carefully,
It's blistered brown.
I count to ten,
*Uno, dos, tres . . .*
And then snap it out
Of the pan. The tortilla
Dances in my hands
As I carry it
To the drainboard,
Where I smear it
With butter,
The yellow ribbon of butter
That will drip
Slowly down my arm
When I eat on the front lawn.
The sparrow will drop
Like fruit
From the tree
To stare at me
With his glassy eyes.
I will rip a piece
For him. He will jump
On his food
And gargle it down,
Chirp once and fly
Back into the wintry tree.

# ODE TO THE SPRINKLER

There is no swimming
Pool on
Our street,
Only sprinklers
On lawns,
The helicopter
Of water
Slicing our legs.
We run through
The sprinkler,
Water on our
Lips, water
Dripping
From eyelashes,
Water like
Fat raindrops
That fall from
Skinny trees when
You're not looking.
I run *como*
*Un chango,*
In my orange
Swimming trunks,
Jumping up and
Down, pounding
The mushy grass
With my feet.
One time a bee
Stung my toe,

The next-to-the-biggest
Toe. Then that toe
Got bigger
Than my real
Big toe,
Like a balloon
On its way up.
I cried and
Sat on the porch.
The water on
My face was not
Water from the sprinkler,
But water from
Inside my body,
Way down where
Pain says, *¡Híjole!*
That hurts!
Mom brought me
A glass of Kool-Aid.
I drank some
And then pressed
The icy glass
Against my throbbing toe.
The toe
Shrank back
Into place,
And on that day
I began to think
Of Kool-Aid not
As sugar on
The tongue
But as medicine.
And as for the bees,

You have to watch
For them. They buzz
The lawn for
Their own sugar
And wet play.

# ODE TO SEÑOR LEAL'S GOAT

In the back yard
With three red
Chickens, the goat
With a tin can
For a bell drinks
From a rain puddle.
The puddle reflects
A blue sky, some clouds,
And the goat's tongue
Darting in and out.
When Señor Leal
Comes down the back
Porch, the goat looks
Up and nods his head.
The bell clangs,
And the chickens
Look up, heads cocked,
Strut and follow
The goat. The goat
Gets a carrot
And the chickens get
Clapping hands
That scare them away.
Chickens go back to
Pecking at the sandy ground.
Señor Leal feeds
His goat, and
Then lights his pipe.
Señor Leal, breathing in,

Looks at the sky,
Blue as an egg,
And feels good.
It's early morning.
The wind from
Some faraway mountain
Has reached him.
Señor Leal inhales
On his pipe
And then admires
The sky some more.
The goat, not knowing
Better, grabs the pipe
From Señor Leal's hand.
Señor Leal yells,
"*¿Qué pasó?*" The goat,
With pipe hanging
From his mouth,
Runs around the yard,
Through the patch
Of chiles and tomatoes,
The purple of
Eggplants. "Hey,"
Señor Leal yells.
The goat can't baa,
Because his lips
Are gripping the pipe —
A funny sight for
The chickens,
Who stay clear.
When Señor Leal
Finally grabs his goat,
The pipe is smoked.

And the goat's eyes
Are spinning from
The dizzy breath
Of man's bad habit.

# ODE TO MI PERRITO

He's brown as water
Over a stone,
Brown as leaves and branches,
Brown as pennies in a hand.
He's brown as my mitt
On a bedpost,
And just as quick:
A baseball rolls
His way and his teeth
Chatter after it.
*Mi perrito* rolls
His tongue for the taste
Of a dropped *chicharrón*,
For the jawbreaker
That fell from my pocket,
For a potato chip bag
Blowing across a lawn.
He's brown as earth
But his days are yellow
As the sun at noon.
Today he rode
In my father's car,
His paws on the dash
As he looked around
At the road giving way
To farms and countryside.
He barked at slow drivers
And Father barked back.
Where did they go?

Fishing. Ten miles
From town, and they crossed
A river, blue with the
Rush of water.
Fish lurked beneath
The surface, the big
O of their mouths
Gulping bubbles.
Father threw his line
There, and waited,
His hands in his pockets.
*Mi perrito* didn't wait.
He jumped into the river,
And jumped back out —
The water was icy
Cold. Father fished
And *mi perrito*
Walked along the riverbank,
Sniffing for birds
And cool-throated mice.
*Mi perrito* was a hunter.
He crept in the low brush,
His ears perked up.
When he jumped,
His paws landed on a cricket.
The cricket chirped
And jumped into
The gray ambush of grass.
He barked and returned
To my father, who
Returned to the car:
The fish would have
Nothing of hook and sinker.

15

They drove back
To town through the curve
Of hills. When
My father turned
Sharply, *mi perrito* barked
Because it's his job
To make noise
Of oncoming danger.
He had his paws
Up on the dash,
With a good view
Of the hills
Where cows sat down on the job.
When one cow dared
To moo, *mi perrito* barked
And showed his flashing teeth.
*Mi perrito* is a chihuahua —
Smaller than a cat,
Bigger than a rubber mouse.
Like mouse and cat,
He goes running
When the real dogs
Come into the yard.

# ODE TO LOS CHICHARRONES

They are shaped
Like trumpets,
The blow of salt
On your lips
When you raise
One to your mouth.
The music is a crunch
On the back molars,
A hard crunch that
Flushes the ears
And tires the jaw.
When Mamá is
Not looking,
When she is stabbing
Your torn pants
With a threaded needle,
You sneak into
The kitchen:
They're on top
Of the refrigerator,
Among the old bread
Sighing in plastic wrappers,
And the forgotten oranges,
Puckered as elbows.
It's the *chicharrones*
That you want,
Salt for football
In the front yard,
Salt for the hoe

You will take up
To clear the flower bed
Before your father comes home,
Salt for the bike race
And the shadow you
Won't catch.
You take a horn
Of *chicharrón,*
And sneak out
Of the house.
The first bite
Is in the alley,
The second bite
In a tree,
The third bite
On a car fender
Of a neighbor who
Has yelled, *"¡Ay, Dios!"*
To the racket
Of *chicharrón*
Being devoured
By adult teeth
In a fourth grader's head.
She tells you to go away,
And you do, walking up
The street with
Your half-bitten horn of plenty,
A dog at your heels.
When you're through,
The dog will lick
Your palms for the flakes
Of oil and salt,
And he will wag

His tail
And pump his legs
In his parade
Of dog happiness.
You drink cool water
From a garden hose
And sit on the lawn,
The sun riding a
White cloud of autumn.
You enjoyed
The trumpet
Of noise and salt.
And even the ants
Raised their heads:
Knowing what's good,
They dropped their bread crumbs
For a single flake
Of *chicharrón*.

# DE TO PABLO'S TENNIS SHOES

They wait under Pablo's bed,
Rain-beaten, sun-beaten,
A scuff of green
At their tips
From when he fell
In the school yard.
He fell leaping for a football
That sailed his way.
But Pablo fell and got up,
Green on his shoes,
With the football
Out of reach.

Now it's night.
Pablo is in bed listening
To his mother laughing
To the Mexican *novelas* on TV.
His shoes, twin pets
That snuggle his toes,
Are under the bed.
He should have bathed,
But he didn't.
(Dirt rolls from his palm,
Blades of grass
Tumble from his hair.)
He wants to be
Like his shoes,
A little dirty
From the road,

A little worn
From racing to the drinking fountain
A hundred times in one day.
It takes water
To make him go,
And his shoes to get him
There. He loves his shoes,
Cloth like a sail,
Rubber like
A lifeboat on rough sea.
Pablo is tired,
Sinking into the mattress.
His eyes sting from
Grass and long words in books.
He needs eight hours
Of sleep
To cool his shoes,
The tongues hanging
Out, exhausted.

# O DE TO LA LLORONA

They say she weeps
Knee-deep in the river,
The gray of dusk
A shawl over her head.
She weeps for her children,
Their smothered faces
Of sleeping angels . . .
Normaaaa, Marioooo, Carloooos.
They say she calls
Children, offering
Them candy
From her sleeve.
They say she will
Point a long finger,
Gnarled root of evilness,
And stare a soft
Hole in your lungs:
The air leaks
From this hole
And climbs in the trees.
In autumn, she appears
With a pomegranate,
Each seed the heart
Of a child she took away.
She will whisper, Monicaaaaa,
Beniciooooo, Ernestooooo.
If you're on your bike,
Ride faster.
If you're on foot,

Run without looking up.
In these times,
The sliced moon hangs
In the sky, moon
That is orange,
The color of
A face in the porchlight.
At home
The cooler in the window
Stops, then starts,
And the TV flickers
With a climate of snow.
These are signs, and the
Dog with mismatched eyes,
The turtle in the
Middle of the road,
And the newspapers
Piling up on a roof.
La Llorona is the mother
Of drowned children.
Beware a woman
Dripping water in July
When no rain has fallen.

# ● DE TO MI PARQUE

On Sundays
After Mass,
After the car
Is washed
And the lawn cut — blades
Of grass standing up
In salute — we go
To the park. We drive
Slowly, warm air sucking
Into the rolled-down windows
Of our Chevy, the
Sharpest one on the block.
As we enter
The park we drive
In circles. Papá
Taps his thumb
Against the horn
When he sees friends
And their families
Gathered around barbecues.
They wave and we wave.
I often think,
They're drinking sodas
And eating chips
Without us.
Papá finds our place.
Parking the car,
He goes back and forth
Until it's just right.

He revs the engine,
A cloud of blue smoke
From the tailpipe,
And cuts it off.
We all pile out
Of the back seat,
Lourdes and María,
And baby Alex
With his Tinkertoys
Wet with drool.
I help Mamá with
The aluminum chairs,
The hibachi, the
Ice chest with
Its treasure of cold, cold ice.

I like looking at fire.
Papá starts the hibachi
With a pile of briquets
And bark from
The eucalyptus,
Those tall trees
They say drink
Like elephants.
Wind shoves smoke in
My face, stinging
My eyes. I blink
And cough. I sneeze
As I get away.
And I like getting away.
I like walking alone
In the park,
A stick in my hand,

Imagining a hundred arrows
In my side.
One time I did
Get lost. I was six then,
A little taller
Than our dog Queenie,
And I walked around
The pink-colored
Restrooms, past the
Monkey bars and
The train tracks,
Where sparrows
Hopped on and off
The shiny rails.
I walked until I
Was lost. When I tried
To get back,
I kept going to
The wrong picnic
Table: the families
Looked like my family,
With lots of kids
And smoke from the hibachi
Stinging everyone's eyes.
When I called, "Mamá! Mamá!"
A woman looked up. Her eyes
Were wet, not from laughter,
But from breathing in smoke.
I don't know how
I got back, but I did.
See, it's a Sunday now
And I'm hot from playing soccer
With my sister. We sit
On the picnic table,

Swinging our legs
And looking for
Something easy to do.
Lourdes, my older sister,
Wants to play
A game, a contest
Of who can keep
A hand in ice.
We throw open
The ice chest,
And counting one, two, three,
Plunge our hands
Into the ice.
Lourdes looks at me,
And I look at her,
And even though we're cold
Sweat beads our brows.
I count thirty-one, thirty-two. . . .
My hand comes up first,
Pink as a starfish,
Then plunges back
Into the ice for cream sodas,
A winner after all.

# ODE TO MI GATO

He's white
As spilled milk,
My cat who sleeps
With his belly
Turned toward
The summer sky.
He loves the sun,
Its warmth like a hand.
He loves tuna cans
And milk cartons
With their dribble
Of milk. He loves
Mom when she rattles
The bag of cat food,
The brown nuggets
Raining into his bowl.
And my cat loves
Me, because I saved
Him from a dog,
Because I dressed him
In a hat and a cape
For Halloween,
Because I dangled
A sock of chicken skin
As he stood on his
Hind legs. I love *mi gato,*
*Porque* I found
Him on the fender
Of an abandoned car.

He was a kitten,
With a meow
Like the rusty latch
On a gate. I carried
Him home in the loop
Of my arms.
I poured milk
Into him, let him
Lick chunks of
Cheese from my palms,
And cooked *huevo*
After *huevo*
Until his purring
Engine kicked in
And he cuddled
Up to my father's slippers.
That was last year.
This spring,
He's excellent at sleeping
And no good
At hunting. At night
All the other cats
In the neighborhood
Can see him slink
Around the corner,
Or jump from the tree
Like a splash of
Milk. We lap up
His love and
He laps up his welcome.

# ODE TO MY LIBRARY

It's small
With two rooms
Of books, a globe
That I once
Dropped, some maps
Of the United States and México,
And a fish tank with
A blue fish that
Is always making *jeta*.
There are tables and chairs,
And a pencil sharpener
On the wall: a crayon is stuck
In it, but I didn't do it.

It's funny, but the
Water fountain
Is cooled by a motor,
And the librarian reads
Books with her
Glasses hanging
From her neck. If she
Put them on
She would see me
Studying the Incas
Who lived two steps
From heaven, way in the mountains.

The place says, "Quiet, please,"
But three birds
Talk to us
Loudly from the window.
What's best is this:
A phonograph
That doesn't work.
When I put on the headphones,
I'm the captain of a jet,
And my passengers
Are *mis abuelitos*
Coming from a dusty ranch
In Monterrey. I want
To fly them to California,
But then walk
Them to my library.
I want to show them
The thirty books I devoured
In the summer read-a-thon.

I want to show them
The mural I helped paint.
In the mural,
An Aztec warrior
Is standing on a mountain
With a machete
And a band of feathers
On his noble head.
I made the cuts
Of muscle on
His stomach
And put a boulder
Of strength in each arm.

He could gather
Enough firewood
With one fist.
He could slice
Open a mountain
With that machete,
And with the wave of his arm
Send our enemies tumbling.

If I could fly,
I would bring
*Mis abuelitos* to California.
They would touch my hair
When I showed
Them my library:
The fish making *jeta,*
The globe that I dropped,
The birds fluttering
Their wings at the window.
They would stand me
Between them,
When I showed them
My thirty books,
And the cuts
On the warrior,
Our family of people.

# ● DE TO LA PIÑATA

It sways
In the tree
In the yard,
This paper pig
Bloated with
Candies, this
*Piñata* my father
Bought and hung
On a low branch.
I'm Rachel.
Today's my birthday.
If six fingers
Go up, that's how
Old I am. I'm going
To strike the
*Piñata* six times,
And then let my
Six guests swing
A broom at the pig.
Dad works the rope.
Mom blindfolds me
With a dish towel
And turns me six times,
My lucky number
For my lucky day.
When she stops,
I keep going,
Dizzy and sick —
Inside my belly

A merry-go-round
Of hot dog, chips,
Pink lemonade,
And cake with ice cream.
I stagger and swing.
I fall to a knee,
Rise, and swing again.
I'm more dizzy
Than when I started,
And then, *wham,*
The stick explodes
Against the *piñata.*
My friends laugh
And squeal, and I hit
It again, the first
Rain of candies.
I pull away
The dish towel, dazed
By the sunlight.
I give the stick
To a friend,
And more candies
Rain to the ground,
Kisses and jawbreakers,
Tootsie Rolls like
Chocolate worms.
My six friends
All take a turn,
And then baby brother
From his stroller
Whacks a plastic bat —
Candies rain down,
And by magic, one falls
Into his squealing mouth.

# ODE TO A DAY IN THE COUNTRY

A dirty cloud of sheep
On the hill,
Their faces
Nibbling grass
Wet with rain.
The sheep drink
And eat, their buds
Of tongues
Gathering up the wet world.
If they looked up,
Their faces would be green
With blades of grass.
If they took a step,
Their hooves would
Bury the ant,
Little pilgrim of crust
And fallen bread.
We love sheep.
We love the fatness
Of wool, the itch
Of something warm to wear.
So man tugs on a sock,
And this is sheep.
So woman puts on a coat,
And this is sheep.
So child slips on a hat,
And this is sheep.

We're closer to the country
Than we think,

39

As close as a snowy fingertip
Of glove on the table,
The frayed knot of a robe
In the closet,
The musty sleeve of a sweater
Sleeping with its arms crossed
In a drawer.
We love these sheep.
They stood for us,
Heavy with wool,
As they moved like a dirty cloud
Over the hill
Where the rain last fell.

# DE TO EL GUITARRÓN

All summer
It has stood
In the closet,
This *guitarrón*
That's as big
As a washtub
Or a fat uncle.
Now that my
Mom and dad are gone,
I take it out
And run a finger
Of dust
From its throat.
I carry it
To the living room.
I place it
Between my legs
Like a cello
And thump
The strings.
Dust shakes
From the lamp.
Dust lets go of
My model airplane
On the TV.
Dust falls from
The ceiling
Where spiders breed
In shadowy corners.
I thump all

42

Five strings and
Scare my cat Negrito,
Who jumps from
The couch and onto
The windowsill
In the kitchen.
When he looks back,
I thump the *guitarrón*
With all the heart
Of five skinny fingers.
The cat falls
Like a paper sack
Of fruit.
I go to the window
And watch Negrito
Race across our lawn
And climb the fence
In two blurry leaps.
I thump some more,
A buzz of music
Rattling my chest.
The neighbor kids
With candies
In their mouths
Come running
To ask, "*¿Qué es?*"
"*Música,*" I tell them
With pride. "Do you want
Another song?" They
Nod their heads yes,
The blood of
Chocolate running
From the corners
Of their mouths.

I breathe in a lot
Of good fresh
Saturday air
And let my
Fingers run like
A wild crab
Across the strings.
The music rattles
The window and
Scares the cat out
Of one of its lives
As it drops
From the fence.
I play so hard
That our deaf neighbor
Señor Martínez
Shudders from
His sleep on the porch
Of fat-eared cacti.
He staggers over,
His cane tapping
The ground.
I notice a leaf
In his hair the color
Of wintry twigs.
His sweater is
Buttoned all wrong
And he could choke himself
If he's not careful.
He says, *"Dámelo,"*
And I hand
Him the *guitarrón*
Through the window.

He starts to thump
The strings
So that the noise
Is real music
And my cat Negrito
Returns to sit
On the fence.
He sings, *"Ay, ay,
Mi vida . . ."*
And the kids
Just stare at him.
They wipe their
Dirty faces
And say, *"Qué bueno."*
Señor Martínez
Staggers back
To his porch
For more sleep.
Negrito claws
His way back
Onto the fence,
His eyes shiny
As marbles.
When I start
To thump the strings
Again, my cat
Falls off, scared.
I think it was his ninth life.
I'll find out later
When I hold out
A fist of cat food
And call
Here, kittykittykitty.

# ODE TO FIREWORKS

On Fourth of July,
When it's not yet dark,
I'm a *diablito*
With a sparkler.
I run around
The yard,
Chasing our rooster,
Who gives up
Feathers and screams.
Then it's my turn
To run around
As my big brother,
With a haircut like devil horns,
Chases me with a firecracker.
"*Ándale,*" he yells,
"I'm gonna blow you up."
Of course, he won't —
He's my brother
And I owe him two bucks.
So we each get
A fistful of sparklers,
Firecrackers,
A paper log cabin
That smokes and fizzes,
Rockets that shower sparks
About the height
Of the clothesline.
We get three seconds
Of pinwheels, whistling banshees,

46

Some cones and pyramids
That stink but won't work,
And black pills
That vomit snakes
Of ash. I touch
The ash, and the snake crumbles
And won't bite. Of course
When we finish,
It's not yet dark.
We're mad for not waiting.
I punch him in the arm
And he punches me back.
We climb onto the roof,
My brother first,
And we watch the sky
For rockets. Planes fly by,
Blinking red lights.
A gnat buzzes my ear.
A TV goes on in the neighbor's house.
We wait and wait,
And then they come —
The fireworks from kids
Who saved up for night.

# DE TO WEIGHT LIFTING

Tony eats apples
On Saturday morning,
Two for each arm,
And one for the backs
Of his calves.
He's twelve
And a weight lifter in his garage.
He bites into an apple,
And, chewing,
He curls weights —
One, two, three . . .
His face reddens,
And a blue vein
Deepens on his neck —
Four, five, six . . .
Sweat inches down
His cheek. A curl of
Hair falls in his face —
Seven, eight, nine . . .
He grunts and strains —
Ten, eleven, twelve!
Tony curls his age,
And he would curl his weight
Of 83 pounds, but he
Would pull a muscle
In his arm.

Tony pulls off his T-shirt.
He flexes his biceps,

And apples show up in his arms.
"Pretty good," he says,
His fists clenched.
He takes another
Bite of apple,
And out of happiness
Bites the apples
In his biceps, tenderly
Of course. The teeth
Marks are pink,
His arms brown,
And his roar red as a lion's
With a paw swiping at air.

# ODE TO WEDDINGS

For María,
It's the lace dress,
The cake with
Its three tiers,
The pink punch
With its armada of ice cubes.
It's the drive from
The church. The horns
Blare from one
Street to the next,
And the paper flowers
Taped to the hoods
Blow in the traffic of wind.

For María's mother
It's the music,
The mariachis
With their
Guitar, trumpets,
And the romance
Of two violins.
It's the hug
From the bride,
And a pat on the arm
From the groom.
It's the gossip
And cups of coffee,
And "*Ay, Dios*"
To rumors of love.

For Pedro,
The little brother,
It's the chicken *mole*,
First on his plate
But soon on his shirt.
He hates the bow tie
And his hair plastered down
With the stink
Of *Abuelo*'s pomade.
He hates his feet
Squeezed into shoes
And the white socks.
He hates that
The bride and groom
Are the first to cut
Into the cake,
Sugar heaven for
The three baby teeth
Still in his head.
His fork has been ready
For one long hour.

For the father,
It's the beer
With his *compadres*,
The four of them
Along the wall,
Their ties undone
And coats open.
They're talking
Baseball. The Dodgers
Up by three,
At the beginning
Of August.

They're worried
About the three-game
Surge by the Giants.
They're worried
About lawns
And new tires,
The burglary
Of a friend's house,
And the bicycle
Snatched from
Someone's boy — or
So they heard.
They're worried
But happy. It's
Been a good year
Of pay raises
And children in college.

It's Saturday
In Los Angeles. The sky
Is almost blue and
A blessed wind
Has cooled the hallway.
The high school *novios*
Are now married,
Belinda and Rudolfo.
When they smile,
The hands of old *tías*
Touch their hearts
And the *viejos* raise
Their half-finished beers
To the slosh of *salud*.
Then the dance music
Starts, slowly at first,

Then wildly, with
Bodies spinning.
A breeze sends
The fancy napkins
On the table
Blowing like flowers.

# ODE TO POMEGRANATES

Just as fall
Turns the air,
And the first
Leaves begin
To parachute
To the ground,
The pomegranate
Bursts a seam
And the jewels
Wink a red message.
The García brothers
Have been waiting.
All summer
They have lived
On candies and plums,
Bunches of grapes
From their *tío*
In the San Joaquin Valley.
Now it's time
On this bright Saturday
When they'll jump
The fence of Mrs. López
And pluck off
Six pomegranates.
It's six sins
Against them,
But they just can't help
Themselves. They
Love that treasure

Of jewels glistening
Through cracked husks.
Sitting at a curb,
The Garcías bite
Into the pomegranates,
And their mouths
Fill with the shattered
Sweetness. The blood
Of the fruit runs
Down to their elbows,
Like a vein,
Like a red river,
Like a trail of red ants.
They eat without talking.
When they finish
With four of the six
Pomegranates,
Their mouths are red.
As the laughter of clowns.
And they are clowns.
Mrs. López has been watching
Them from the windows.
She can see that they
Are boys who live
By the sweet juice on tongues.
From her porch,
She winds up
Like a pitcher
And hurls a pomegranate.
It splatters
In the road,
A few inches from them,
The juice flying up

Like blood.
The boys run down
The street,
With shame smeared
On their dirty faces.

# ODE TO EL MOLCAJETE

It's a stone
In my *abuela*'s kitchen,
A stone which
Grinds Fresno chiles
And runs with
The blood of tomatoes.
The half moon of onion
Cries sad tears
Into the stone,
And my *abuela*
Leaks two or three tears,
Not from the sadness
Of a son going away,
Not for the starstruck
Young couples
In TV *novelas.*
It's the onion
That makes her cry.
She wipes a tear
With a crushed Kleenex
And waves a hand
Over her nose,
The fumes of the chile
Lifting toward the ceiling.

Once, I licked
A spoon still puddled
In the *molcajete*,
And I ran around

The back yard,
My tongue like a red flag,
Like the tongue
Of a dog on a hot day.
I drank from
The hose, a gas station
Of water filling up
My one-gallon stomach.

Another time
I took *molcajete*
To the back yard.
I filled it
With wet dirt,
This upside-down turtle,
This slaughterhouse
For chiles and tomatoes,
The thousand sheets of onion.
But it wasn't the onion
That made me cry,
But my mother
Looking out from the window.
She tapped the glass
And pointed an angry finger
At the *molcajete*,
Packed with dirt
And sprouting a forest
Of twigs and popsicle sticks.

I don't know
How my *abuelo* does it,
Spoons the fire
Of chile
Onto his *frijoles*,

And scoops them up
With tortilla.
I stand by him when
He eats. To me,
The chile is a gush
Of lava. But
His jaw goes up
And down, and my mouth
Goes up and
Down, on red candy,
The best I can do.
When I pass
The kitchen,
I pet the *molcajete,*
The turtle-shaped stone
That could snap
Your tongue
And make it wag
Crowns of fire.

# ODE TO FAMILY PHOTOGRAPHS

This is the pond, and these are my feet.
This is the rooster, and this is more of my feet.

*Mamá was never good at pictures.*

This is a statue of a famous general who lost an arm,
And this is me with my head cut off.

This is a trash can chained to a gate,
This is my father with his eyes half-closed.

This is a photograph of my sister
And a giraffe looking over her shoulder.

This is our car's front bumper.
This is a bird with a pretzel in its beak.
This is my brother Pedro standing on one leg on a rock,
With a smear of chocolate on his face.

*Mamá sneezed when she looked*
*Behind the camera: the snapshots are blurry,*
*The angles dizzy as a spin on a merry-go-round.*

But we had fun when Mamá picked up the camera.
How can I tell?
Each of us laughing hard.
Can you see? I have candy in my mouth.

# ODE TO THE MAYOR

Dear Mayor,
My brother Danny
Chipped his tooth
On the cracked sidewalk,
His fault really
Because he was on
His skateboard
With his eyes closed
And his fat mouth open.
His front tooth
Is chipped.
Now he sticks
His tongue
Where his tooth was.
He's making me mad.
He's making my baby sister mad,
Because she was the one
Missing a tooth,
My fault because
I was racing her around
In the stroller
And tipped her over
Taking a corner.
No cracked sidewalk
There, just flat,
Smooth sidewalk.

Dear Mayor,
I'm writing you

Not about my sister
But about Danny.
He's bothering everybody.
He's on his board
Right now and he's
Taunting three girls,
His fat tongue
Wiggling like a worm
From the chipped place
In his mouth.
It's embarrassing.
No one likes us.
Not even dogs come by
To wag their tails.

Dear Mayor,
Have you seen Danny
When you drive
Around town?
He wears glasses.
Sometimes he wears
A T-shirt,
And sometimes
He doesn't,
Brown face
Sticky with ice cream.
Mom cut his
Hair yesterday
And he's bald
As a fist.
Just look for
A waggling tongue.
Is there a law

Against a boy
With glasses,
Sticky face,
No hair,
And a tongue
Between his teeth
On a Saturday morning?

# SPANISH WORDS AND PHRASES

*abuela*   grandmother
*abuelo*   grandfather
*abuelitos*   grandparents
*ándale*   hurry up
*ay, ay, mi vida*   oh, oh, my life
*ay, Dios*   oh, God
*chicharrones*   fried pork rinds
*el cielo es azul*   the sky is blue
*como un chango*   like a monkey
*compadres*   very close friends
*dámelo*   give it to me
*diablito*   little devil
*frijoles*   refried beans
*gato*   cat
*guitarrón*   acoustic bass guitar
*helados*   ice cream
*híjole*   exclamation as in, "Wow!"
*huevo*   egg
*jeta*   thick lips, as in pouting
*la Llorona*   the weeping woman
*molcajete*   mortar for grinding herbs and spices
*novelas*   soap operas
*novios*   lovers
*perrito*   doggie
*porque*   because
*qué bueno*   how good
*¿qué es?*   what is it?
*¿qué pasó?*   what happened?

*raspados*   snow cones
*salud*   cheers
*tía*   aunt
*tío*   uncle
*viejos*   old men